Expedition

Following Jesus on a Mast-Raising,
Sail-Setting, and Treasure-Seeking Journey
to the Ends of the Earth

Incipiosermo Press   incipiosermo.com

Expedition: Following Jesus on a Mast-Raising, Sail-Setting, and Treasure-Seeking Journey to the Ends of the Earth

Scriptures taken from the Holy Bible, New International Version®, NIV®. Copyright © 1973, 1978, 1984, 2011 by Biblica, Inc.™ Used by permission of Zondervan. All rights reserved worldwide. www.zondervan.com The "NIV" and "New International Version" are trademarks registered in the United States Patent and Trademark Office by Biblica, Inc.™

© 2017 Bryce Ashlin-Mayo

Bryce Ashlin-Mayo
bryceashlinmayo.com
bryce@bryceashlinmayo.com

© Second edition - January 2021

ISBN: 978-1-9994741-2-6 (print)
ISBN: 978-1-9994741-3-3 (electronic)

Incipiosermo Press
incipiosermo.com

ACKNOWLEDGEMENTS

Thank you to all those who helped make this book possible. Thank you to Laurie Ashlin-Mayo for skillfully editing the prose, to Ken Born for your graphic design and expertise to make it visually beautiful, and to all those who read and gave thoughtful feedback.

PREFACE

Congratulations!

The fact that you are reading this book likely means that you have recently chosen, in faith, to follow Jesus on His great expedition. As a result of your decision, your life has been made new and has been given a new purpose and a new mission. In Jesus, you have been given abundant and eternal life. That is exciting and worth celebrating!

When someone decides to follow Jesus, they are often faced with many questions, wondering what to do next. This book aims to help guide the first steps on that journey using the image and metaphor of an expeditionary sailing ship.

As a follower of Jesus, you are now on a treasure-seeking expeditionary vessel with Jesus as its captain, His followers as its crew, the mast and boom as foundational to its purpose, the sail as its means of power, the Bible as its rudder, prayer as its form of communication, and heaven as its final port of call. Consistent with how the Bible views our faith, it is simultaneously a personal and a collective expedition. By design, you are not on your faith journey alone and you need others in your journey as you follow Jesus, surrender to the Holy Spirit, and participate in His mission.

"Life is either an adventure or nothing."
~ Helen Keller

As you will soon discover, following Jesus on His expedition is a lifelong pursuit with much to learn as you follow Him. As a simple introduction to that relationship and mission, I trust this is a helpful guide as you join with others in following Jesus on His mast-raising, sail-setting, and treasure-seeking journey to the ends of the earth.

The expedition awaits...

Recommended Resources and Steps to Sail Further in the Voyage of Faith

All expeditionary vessels have a space called a "hold" where they store extra resources for the journey. This book also includes a "hold" at the end of each chapter to help you sail further in the voyage of faith. Each "hold" section may include a recommended book resource, an online resource, and/or an action step. Although Jesus transforms us, we are active participants as we learn, grow, and submit more of ourselves to Him.

> "If you want to build a ship, don't drum up the men to gather wood, divide the work and give orders. Instead, teach them to yearn for the vast and endless sea."
>
> ~ Antoine de Saint-Exupery, "The Wisdom of the Sands"

EMBARKATION

Following Jesus means we have embarked on a journey and boarded Jesus' expeditionary vessel. Embarking on that journey means that we have placed our belief in Jesus, crossed the gunnel (edge of the ship) in faith, and boarded His ship. Crossing that threshold and boarding the expeditionary vessel is an act of belief and faith.

Belief and Faith

As a young adult, I worked at a summer camp teaching canoeing to underprivileged and behaviourally challenged children. It was a great challenge and tremendous opportunity that I enjoyed immensely. At the beginning of each new canoeing lesson, I would teach my young urban students the basics of the canoe and paddle. Learning the names of different parts of the boat and the simple mechanics of how to paddle while on the safety of the shore were key to the next step of getting my young students on the water and safely afloat.

As we progressed through the training process, they would learn a number of things on shore that were necessary for canoeing. However, unless they were willing to get in the boat, it would only be a lesson in belief devoid of any faith. Believing a canoe can hold you and that it is possible to navigate it forward is one thing, but having the faith needed to move beyond the safety of shore, trusting in the boat's ability to keep you afloat is something different altogether.

Following Jesus takes both belief and faith. To embark and board the ship of faith, one must believe that Jesus is the Son of God who lived a perfect life and died and rose again from the dead.[1] Belief in who Jesus is and what He has done is key and important, but it is not the only thing needed for the expedition God wants us to be a part of. We also need faith.[2] Faith is the act of putting one's belief into action. It is having faith that Jesus, the Son of God, is our only hope for salvation. Faith is expressing our need for Jesus by confessing our wrongs, intentionally turning from them in repentance and receiving the forgiveness freely offered in Jesus. We can't have faith in a boat from the safety of the shore. We can only have faith in a boat while aboard, floating on the water.

This is the invitation of Jesus. Jesus invites us aboard His ship in belief and faith on His expedition of love. To cross the threshold of the gunnel is an act of belief and faith where we ask Jesus to be our Saviour and make Him the Captain of our life.[3]

Baptism

As people who have embarked on Jesus' expeditionary mission in faith, Jesus calls us to be baptized as an outward declaration of our inward transformation. Baptism is the sacred act of declaring to the world our decision to follow Jesus with our lives and to participate with Him on His expedition of love. To that end, the Christian rite of baptism has been instituted and demonstrated by Jesus and practiced for millennia. In our stream of Christianity, baptism is practiced by being fully immersed in water. In other words, baptism is the symbolic act that we have died to our sin by going under the water and are now alive in Jesus when we come up out of the water. In this,

---

[1] Romans 10:9-10 "If you declare with your mouth, "Jesus is Lord," and believe in your heart that God raised him from the dead, you will be saved. For it is with your heart that you believe and are justified, and it is with your mouth that you profess your faith and are saved."

[2] Hebrew 11:1 "Now faith is confidence in what we hope for and assurance about what we do not see."

[3] Romans 10:9 "If you declare with your mouth, "Jesus is Lord," and believe in your heart that God raised him from the dead, you will be saved."

we symbolically profess our participation in both the death and resurrection of Jesus, finding our new life in Him.[4]

Importantly, baptism is something that Jesus specifically asks all His followers to do. Baptism is not an optional practice for faithfully following Jesus but an act of obedience to Jesus' calling and instruction.

Biblically, the only requirement for baptism is a decision to follow Jesus, the understanding of baptism, and a desire to publicly proclaim that decision to the world.[5] Therefore, once you have decided to follow Jesus, your next decision is baptism. To that end, you don't need to have everything figured out, your life doesn't have to be perfect, and your world doesn't have to be "all together." Like salvation, baptism is not about what you have done but what Jesus has done for you. It is the public proclamation that you have joined, in faith, in Jesus' death and resurrection and are committed to His life and mission.[6]

Therefore, if you are not baptized, what is holding you back?

If you have boarded Jesus' expeditionary ship in faith, there is nothing stopping you from publicly declaring it.[7] Talk to someone today about being baptized! God wants to use it to move you forward in your faith journey on His great expedition.

---

[4] Romans 6:3-5 "Or don't you know that all of us who were baptized into Christ Jesus were baptized into his death? We were therefore buried with him through baptism into death in order that, just as Christ was raised from the dead through the glory of the Father, we too may live a new life. For if we have been united with him in a death like his, we will certainly also be united with him in a resurrection like his."

[5] Acts 8:26-40

[6] Matthew 28:19-20 "Therefore go and make disciples of all nations, baptizing them in the name of the Father and of the Son and of the Holy Spirit, and teaching them to obey everything I have commanded you. And surely I am with you always, to the very end of the age."

[7] Acts 2:38 "Peter replied, "Repent and be baptized, every one of you, in the name of Jesus Christ for the forgiveness of your sins. And you will receive the gift of the Holy Spirit." "

THE HOLD

Recommended Resources and Steps to Sail Further in the Voyage of Faith

1) ACTION STEP: Get Baptized. If you are a follower of Jesus and you have not been baptized, talk to your small group leader or pastor today. This is the next important step in your journey of faith.

Expedition: Following Jesus on a Mast-Raising, Sail-Setting, and Treasure-Seeking Journey to the Ends of the Earth

RAISING THE MAST

The decision to follow Jesus has significant implications and an important calling. To follow Jesus means that your entire life is now defined by an all-encompassing expedition.[8]

As followers of Jesus, we have been given a great command by God: "'Love the Lord your God with all your heart and with all your soul and with all your mind and with all your strength.' The second is this: 'Love your neighbour as yourself.'" (Mark 12:30-31a)

Jesus invites us to raise the mast and boom of our lives by articulating the two directions of love on His great expedition.

---

[8] Romans 12:1-2 "Therefore, I urge you, brothers and sisters, in view of God's mercy, to offer your bodies as a living sacrifice, holy and pleasing to God—this is your true and proper worship. Do not conform to the pattern of this world, but be transformed by the renewing of your mind. Then you will be able to test and approve what God's will is—his good, pleasing and perfect will."

Expedition: Following Jesus on a Mast-Raising, Sail-Setting, and Treasure-Seeking Journey to the Ends of the Earth

"I have decided to stick with love. Hate is too great a burden to bear."

~ Martin Luther King Jr.

The first direction is vertical with the raising of our masts to love God with all our heart, mind, soul, and strength. In essence, to love God with all that we are at all times. Importantly, this love is possible because it is a reflective and reciprocal love. We love God because He first loved us.[9] We don't love God in the hope that He will love us back, we love because we are already radically and profoundly loved. We raise the mast because God has lowered it to us through Jesus' life, death, and resurrection.

In addition to the mast, Jesus calls us to secure and extend our boom on the horizontal direction of our lives. Not only are we commanded to love God, we are commanded to love others, even our enemies.[10]

---

[9] 1 John 4:19 "We love because he first loved us."
[10] Matthew 5:44 "But I tell you, love your enemies and pray for those who persecute you,"

Therefore, as followers of Jesus, we do not remove ourselves from our non-Christian friends but endeavour to be their friends in renewed and transformative ways. With God's help, we love our friends with God's selfless love. Also, with intentionality, we love others who are difficult to love. We love those who annoy us, those who have betrayed us, and those who would want to harm us. We love them with a counter-cultural and expansive love that defies explanation apart from Jesus.[11] If those we love on the horizontal plane look like us and act like us then all this tells us is that we love ourselves. It is when we love beyond ourselves that we discover how far our love can take us on God's great expedition.

Just as our masts are called to be increasingly reaching upwards, our booms are to be intentionally reaching outwards. It is in that reaching up and reaching out in love that we build a mast and boom to set a sail upon.

Carrying Our Cross of Love

When you raise both your mast and boom, you form a cross that, as a follower of Jesus, you are called to carry daily in your life. Jesus said "Whoever wants to be my disciple must deny themselves and take up their cross daily and follow me" (Luke 9:23).

If you have decided to follow Jesus, He is calling you to daily pick up your cross, as He did His, and follow Him. To love God with all that you are, and to love everyone, including your enemies, as you love yourself.

---

[11] 1 Corinthians 13:4-8a "Love is patient, love is kind. It does not envy, it does not boast, it is not proud. It does not dishonour others, it is not self-seeking, it is not easily angered, it keeps no record of wrongs. Love does not delight in evil but rejoices with the truth. It always protects, always trusts, always hopes, always perseveres. Love never fails. But where there are prophecies, they will cease; where there are tongues, they will be stilled; where there is knowledge, it will pass away."

This is not a simple ask but one that demands your entire life and extends to every relationship, situation, and circumstance.

Sound impossible? It is! At least, on your own strength. Hence the need for the sail to be unfurled to the mast and boom.

Recommended Resources and Steps to Sail Further in the Voyage of Faith

1) BOOK RESOURCE: "Crazy Love" by Francis Chan

2) ACTION STEP: Intentionally get to know someone different than you and ask God to help you love and serve them. Seek practical ways to demonstrate your love for them outside of your natural capacity, discovering how God will empower you to love beyond yourself.

SETTING THE SAIL

Now that you have embarked on the expedition, raised the mast, and extended the boom, it is time to set the sail. Every sailing ship relies on harnessing the power of the wind to move. Tethered to the mast and the boom, the sail is lifted and propels the ship with the power of the wind. Without wind, traditional ships are left aimlessly adrift in the water.

The Wind

One of the biblical metaphors for the Holy Spirit is wind.[12] The Bible uses wind to symbolize the person and work of the Holy Spirit. As followers of Jesus, we need the Holy Spirit to empower us for life and mission. This same relationship exists between sailing vessels and wind. If a sailing ship is to move anywhere,

---

[12] John 3:8 "The wind blows wherever it pleases. You hear its sound, but you cannot tell where it comes from or where it is going. So it is with everyone born of the Spirit."

"God provides the wind, Man must raise the sail."
~ Augustine of Hippo

it needs to submit to the wind. It must set its sail to effectively traverse the waters.

It may seem like it's an obvious assertion that every sailboat wants to move but, in the metaphor of our lives, too often we are content with drifting afloat in aimless atrophy and missional disengagement.

We were not created to idly float adrift on an ocean of possibility and adventure. Rather, we were created for discovery and exploration. As followers of Jesus, we have been given a sail to propel us on mission, even in the harshest of storms. When our sails are attached to the mast and boom of the great commandment and we surrender to the wind of the Spirit, it will propel us forward on God's great expeditionary mission to make followers of Jesus from all nations.[13]

The Sails

When we come to faith in Jesus, we become a dwelling place of the Holy Spirit in the same way a sail is a vessel of the wind.[14] On Jesus' expedition we are given a sail to be raised (distinct event) and continually filled (progressive experience) with the wind of the Holy Spirit.

The sail we are given purposely looks and acts much like a flag of surrender. Being filled with the Holy Spirit is a conscious and humble act of surrendering to the Lordship of Jesus and the control of the Holy Spirit in all areas of our lives. As we lift our flag of surrender, tethering it to the mast and boom of our love for God and our love for others, we unleash a sail poised to be filled with the Spirit.

Consequently, being filled with the Holy Spirit is not about trying harder but about trusting and surrendering more. We don't have to coax the Holy Spirit to fill us, as if God is reluctant unless we beg hard enough or ask long enough. It is God's will for us to be continually filled, but we struggle with surrendering all of our lives to Him.[15]

Too often, in a prideful attempt to control God and dictate His direction, we strive to blow into our own sails until we hyperventilate in exhaustion. Sadly, churches are filled with exhausted Christians who have tried to hyperventilate their way to transformation and Spirit empowerment. As a result, churches are in desperate need of the freedom that surrendering to the wind of the Spirit will bring. When we surrender to the Spirit, we are transformed and propelled in love.

---

[13] Acts 1:8 "But you will receive power when the Holy Spirit comes on you; and you will be my witnesses in Jerusalem, and in all Judea and Samaria, and to the ends of the earth."

[14] Ephesians 1:13b-14

[15] Ephesians 5:8b "...be filled with the Spirit"

If your Christian life is not going anywhere, if you are not moving forward on mission, if your life is not defined by love, joy, peace, forbearance, kindness, goodness, faithfulness, gentleness, and self-control, and if you are not seeing God at work through you, the answer is not found in trying harder.[16] It is found in surrendering more. It is found in being surrendered to Jesus and being filled with the Holy Spirit. Following Jesus faithfully is impossible without being filled with the Holy Spirit.

Surrender your life to Jesus today. On Jesus' great expedition, He is inviting you to raise your sail, be filled with the Holy Spirit, and experience His power, presence, and purpose on mission with Him.

THE HOLD

Recommended Resources and Steps to Sail Further in the Voyage of Faith

1) BOOK RESOURCE: "How to be Filled with the Holy Spirit" by A.W. Tozer

2) ACTION STEP: Write on cue cards areas of your life that you need to surrender to Jesus. Then, one-by-one, surrender them to Him asking Him to fill you with His Holy Spirit. By raising the white flag of surrender, ask God to fill it with His Spirit (wind) and empower you. Share your desire to be filled with the Holy Spirit with others and have them lay hands on you and pray for you.

---

[16] Galatians 5:16, 22-23 "So I say, walk by the Spirit, and you will not gratify the desires of the flesh...the fruit of the Spirit is love, joy, peace, forbearance, kindness, goodness, faithfulness, gentleness and self-control..."

USING MORSE CODE

Now that you have embarked, raised your mast and boom, and set your sails in surrender, it is time to learn to communicate for a successful expedition. Any effective sailor needs to learn to communicate for successful navigation. To that end, on any modern-day expedition, it would be wise to learn Morse Code.

Morse Code

Morse Code was first invented in the nineteenth-century. It was originally created as a way to communicate with a coded system of an audio form of dots and dashes over the newly invented telegraph and radio as a means to send and receive simple messages. Using this simple system of dots and dashes, messages could be encoded by the sender, sent, and then decoded by the receiver for effective, yet simple, communication across distances.

Expedition: Following Jesus on a Mast-Raising, Sail-Setting, and Treasure-Seeking Journey to the Ends of the Earth

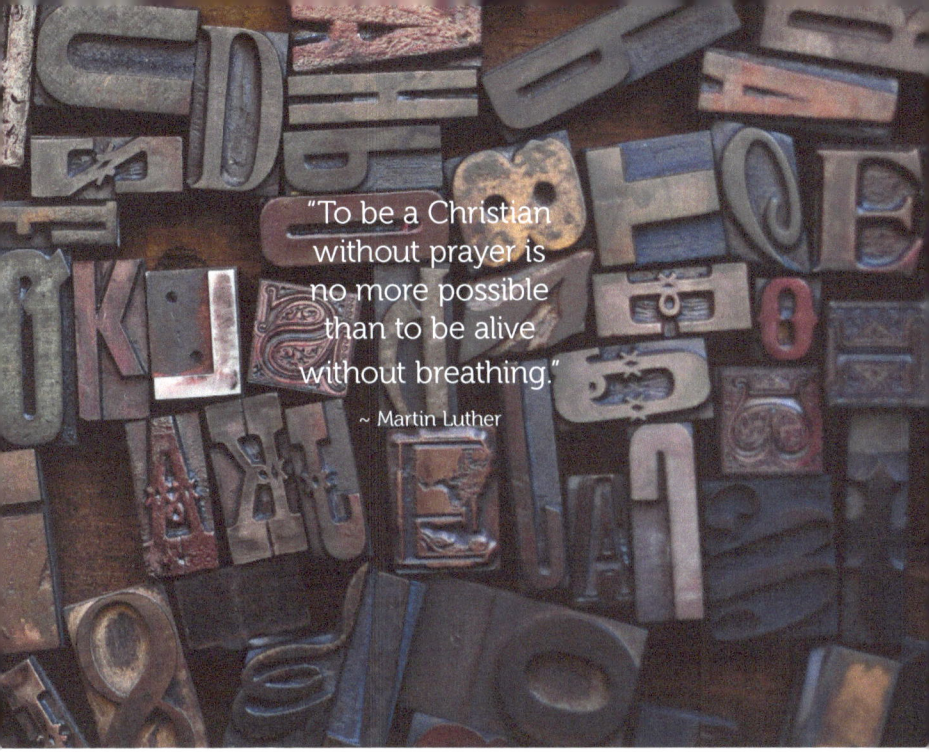

> "To be a Christian without prayer is no more possible than to be alive without breathing."
> ~ Martin Luther

Just as Morse Code is important for ships and their crew, prayer is vital for the success and life of any follower of Jesus. Prayer is simply communicating with God, but like all new forms of communication it takes some time and practice as we learn to do it naturally. Simply, prayer is talking with God as you would talk with a friend (a friend who is also a loving father and powerful king). To help make praying as natural as possible, it is important to remember that we are invited to pray in the Spirit, pray constantly, and pray intentionally.

Pray in the Spirit

The Bible invites us to pray in the Spirit.[17] In other words, the Holy Spirit (God Himself) wants to help us pray.

I remember when our son Lucas was born and had some complications that eventually led to the revelation that he has Down Syndrome. This experience drew me to my knees in desperate prayers that I did not know how to pray. I was lost in finding words for our situation that seemed so overwhelming. What would this mean? How would this change our lives? Did we have what it would take to parent Lucas effectively? Yet through that time God helped me to pray. I remember not knowing how to express the deep questions in my aching heart and yet God met me, loved me, and helped me to not just make it through the season but to experience deep intimate communication with Him through it.

As you learn to pray, simply ask God to help. Ask God to teach you how to pray. Ask God to help express your heart to Him and take increasingly deeper steps of intimacy with Him. As you do, God will help you and mature you as a pray-er.

Pray Constantly

The Bible also invites us to pray constantly.[18] This may seem overwhelming because we have reduced our understanding of prayer to that which we do before meals, before bed, or when we are in desperate trouble. If this is the limited way we understand prayer, then it is impossible to pray like this continually. However, what if prayer is bigger and more beautiful than this? What if prayer is intended to be a constant conversation with a God who is always present?

---

[17] Jude 20-21 "But you, dear friends, by building yourselves up in your most holy faith and praying in the Holy Spirit, keep yourselves in God's love as you wait for the mercy of our Lord Jesus Christ to bring you to eternal life. Romans 8:26 "In the same way, the Spirit helps us in our weakness. We do not know what we ought to pray for, but the Spirit himself intercedes for us through wordless groans."

[18] 1 Thessalonians 5:16-18 "Rejoice always, pray continually, give thanks in all circumstances; for this is God's will for you in Christ Jesus."

On any expeditionary sailing vessel, communication is key and it is constant. The captain is constantly communicating with the crew and the crew is constantly communicating with the captain.[19] Prayer does not have to be reduced to specific times and places but can be a constant part of our day as we continually pray to our God who is constantly with us.

Pray Intentionally

The Bible also invites us to pray intentionally and Jesus teaches us how to do so specifically through the Lord's Prayer (Matthew 6:9-13). The Lord's Prayer is a fantastic framework as part of our intentional and regular prayer lives.

> *"Our Father in heaven, hallowed be your name."* Spend time adoring and worshipping God for who He is. This posture will put the rest of our prayers into perspective. Knowing that Jesus is all-powerful, all-knowing, and ever-present helps makes our prayers bolder and more visceral. We are not bringing our prayers to an impotent God but an all-powerful one.

> *"Your kingdom come, your will be done, on earth as it is in heaven."* Spend time realigning your heart to pray for God's kingdom to come, rather than your own. We can struggle with bringing our agenda, plan, budget, and timetable to God for His blessing and affirmation rather than bringing our life in humble submission to wherever, whenever, and whatever God wants to do with it. God's plan is always better than ours, and we need to regularly realign our hearts to be in submission to His. As we bring our entire lives in surrender to Him, God promises that we will know His good and perfect will.[20]

---

[19] John 10:27 "My sheep listen to my voice; I know them, and they follow me."

[20] Romans 12:1-2 "Therefore, I urge you, brothers and sisters, in view of God's mercy, to offer your bodies as a living sacrifice, holy and pleasing to God—this is your true and proper worship. Do not conform to the pattern of this world, but be transformed by the renewing of your mind. Then you will be able to test and approve what God's will is—his good, pleasing and perfect will."

"Give us today our daily bread." Now that we have recognized who God is and submitted to His will, God invites us to bring our needs to Him. This is not something to be shy about but boldly bring our needs, worries, and stresses to Him. It is also important to identify a key pronoun in this phrase that is often overlooked in our individualistic and selfish world. The Lord's Prayer says, "our daily bread." The "our" here is plural and therefore not just about us individually. It is about our families, our friends, and even our enemy's needs. God invites us to bring all of these needs to him daily.

"And forgive us our debts, as we also have forgiven our debtors. And lead us not into temptation, but deliver us from the evil one." Spend time confessing your sins.[21] Ask God to search your heart and show you anything you need to confess.[22] This isn't necessarily about being comprehensive, but about reorienting our hearts back to God and reminding ourselves of the forgiveness we have in Jesus. Once you have confessed, remind yourself that you are forgiven. This should be a time filled with joy. Thank God for His forgiveness and ask God to lead you out of temptation and help you to forgive those who have hurt you.[23]

Conclude the prayer where it began, with worship and thanksgiving for God is the one with all the power and authority.[24] Start and end with a submission of

---

[21] 1 John 1:9 "If we confess our sins, he is faithful and just and will forgive us our sins and purify us from all unrighteousness."

[22] Psalm 139:23-24 "Search me, God, and know my heart; test me and know my anxious thoughts. See if there is any offensive way in me, and lead me in the way everlasting."

[23] 1 Corinthians 10:13 "No temptation has overtaken you except what is common to mankind. And God is faithful; he will not let you be tempted beyond what you can bear. But when you are tempted, he will also provide a way out so that you can endure it."

[24] 2 Chronicles 20:21 "After consulting the people, Jehoshaphat appointed men to sing to the Lord and to praise him for the splendour of his holiness as they went out at the head of the army, saying: "Give thanks to the Lord, for his love endures forever." "

Expedition: Following Jesus on a Mast-Raising, Sail-Setting, and Treasure-Seeking Journey to the Ends of the Earth

Jesus' Lordship over all things in our lives. This aids in a powerful realignment of our mind and heart to God's authority and will.

The Captain is Speaking

We often consider prayer as us talking to Jesus, but intimacy is never fostered in any relationship with one-way communication. Listening is important to any form of communication and the development of any relationship. God desires to talk to us and does so through the Bible, but also through the Holy Spirit who wants to actively lead us.[25] God can speak through a situation, an impression, the Bible, or even, potentially, audibly. God wants to speak to us and does so by reminding us who we are in Him, convicting us, correcting us, and guiding us in our lives.

As we learn to listen to the voice of God in our lives, may we do so by testing everything we hear with the Bible and with others in community. God never contradicts Himself and often uses others to help us discern His voice. If you think God is communicating something very specific to you, especially pertaining to a decision or action to take, I encourage you to discuss it with other mature believers; God may choose to use them to either bring confirmation or caution to what you believe you have received.

As a follower of Jesus, learning to pray takes practice but it isn't complicated. Pray in the Spirit, pray constantly, and pray intentionally. Learn to pray and continue to practice. Learning to pray will help you hear the voice of the Captain who is leading you on His glorious expeditionary mission.

---

[25] 2 Timothy 3:16-17 "All Scripture is God-breathed and is useful for teaching, rebuking, correcting and training in righteousness, so that the servant of God may be thoroughly equipped for every good work." John 10:27 "My sheep listen to my voice; I know them, and they follow me."

THE HOLD

Recommended Resources and Steps to Sail Further in the Voyage of Faith

1) BOOK RESOURCE: "Prayer: Experiencing Awe and Intimacy with God" by Timothy Keller

2) ONLINE RESOURCE: www.pray-as-you-go.org

3) ACTION STEP: Begin by spending ten minutes per day in prayer using the Lord's Prayer as your guide.

> "Most people are willing to take the Sermon on the Mount as a flag to sail under, but few will use it as a rudder by which to steer."
> ~ Oliver Wendell Holmes

USING THE RUDDER

There is a famous story about an armada of ships participating in military exercises.[26] As they were practicing attack and defence techniques, a thick layer of fog covered the sea like a cold wet blanket making navigation extremely difficult. As one of the seaman took watch, looking for the lights of the other ships in the armada, he witnessed a light peeking through the fog. The light was right in line with the heading of the ship so he called out, in desperation, to the captain. The captain responded, giving directions to the seaman to send a Morse Code message via flashing light to the ship in the distance to turn thirty degrees as they were on a collision course.

Moments later, a coded message returned and the seaman relayed the message to the captain. The other vessel responded: "Collision imminent, turn immediately to avoid."

---

[26] Adapted from Paul Aiello, Jr., Leadership, Vol. 4, no. 2. www.preachingtoday.com/illustrations/1995/august/1033.html

The captain indignantly sent a message in response "We are a battleship, change course immediately."

After what seemed like an eternity, the distant light flashed a message in return: "We are a lighthouse!"

In many ways, this highlights our need for clear direction in the darkness and difficulties we face. Too often, we assume we are correct and on course and our pre-existing beliefs and perception of direction are never questioned.

If we assume that everything we know is absolutely correct and without error, we would be ignoring the history of the human race. History is filled with examples of people who were absolutely convinced of their position, idea, and perspective, even to the point of great sacrifice and great cost, only to be proven wrong over time. As we approach our lives and how we navigate the moral and ethical realities of our world, we need to do so with great humility. To put it plainly, we could be wrong about some of the understandings and ethical decisions we are presently convinced are true.

The same reality extends to our culture's view in following our hearts. There is a pervasive belief that we should just follow our heart, as our heart will never lead us astray. However, a simple self-reflection will lead us to question that belief. As experience often dictates, our hearts do not always lead us to truth or goodness. The Bible teaches this reality when it says: "The heart is deceitful above all things" (Jeremiah 17:9a). Our hearts can mislead us and it is vital that we ask God to realign not only what we believe intellectually but also the direction and pull of our hearts.[27]

This is why the Bible is so important and why we view it as our only rule of faith and practice.[28] It is our guide and source of truth. It is God's Word for us. It is the story of God at work in our world.

The Rudder as God's Story

In many ways, the Bible is like the rudder for our ship. We need to know God's story to guide our story. We need to know the Bible to know what God would want and call us to. The love story of the Bible is the rudder for our mission of love in the world. Without knowing that story and what God would tell us about who He is, what He has done, and the trajectory of history, we are aimless in the water. But with the rudder of the Bible, we can traverse the shifting current of culture, morality, and ethics in our world with confidence and truth.[29]

The Bible bears witness to the truth of Jesus' redemptive plan in the world and how we can be a part of it. It shares how we are to love effectively, live boldly, and share God's love courageously.

---

[27] Psalm 51:10 "Create in me a pure heart, O God, and renew a steadfast spirit within me."

[28] 2 Timothy 3:16-17 "All Scripture is God-breathed and is useful for teaching, rebuking, correcting and training in righteousness, so that the servant of God may be thoroughly equipped for every good work."

[29] Psalm 119

The pages of the Bible are God's constant direction and truth that guides us in the shifting currents of our ever-changing world.

If we want to effectively navigate the rough waters in the changing tide of culture, we need to be reading, memorizing, and meditating on the Bible.[30] The Bible provides life and truth to us and helps to steer us on our expedition of love.

Using the Rudder to Help Steer Your Life

Use the rudder of the expeditionary ship by reading some of the Bible on a daily basis, memorize some important and key verses, and meditate on it. The Bible is a collection of books, songs, poems, and letters, inspired by God and written by many people over hundreds of years. Like all epic stories and histories, it has an overall story arch that, in this case, culminates with Jesus.

For those unfamiliar with the Bible, there are a couple of important things to know. First, the Bible was written in ancient Hebrew, ancient Greek, and ancient Aramaic and, thus, any version we read will be a translation. As a new follower of Jesus, a suggestion is to choose a translation that is easy to read and understand. The *New International Version* (NIV) or the *New Living Translation* (NLT) are popular examples of this.

Second, the Bible is divided into two testaments: the Old Testament and the New Testament. The phrasing of "old" and "new" is an unfortunate misnomer in that "old" is often viewed as meaning outdated and unimportant and "new" meaning better. This is not the case. The Old Testament is largely written in Hebrew and covers God's story to the time of Jesus (the appearance of whom, the Old Testament looks forward to with great expectation). The New Testament is largely written in Greek and covers God's story from the time of Jesus onwards and includes the prophetic foretelling of the future when God will

---

[30] Psalm 1:1-3 "Blessed is the one who does not walk in step with the wicked or stand in the way that sinners take or sit in the company of mockers, but whose delight is in the law of the Lord, and who meditates on his law day and night. That person is like a tree planted by streams of water, which yields its fruit in season and whose leaf does not wither—whatever they do prospers."

make all thing new (the distant shore the expedition is ultimately headed towards). Consequently, both testaments (old and new) are key and important parts of God's story and equally God's Word in every way.

Although not in the original form, our contemporary Bible uses chapters (the large numbers on the page) and verses (small numbers on the page) to help the reader navigate and easily find specific segments of the Bible. This is why, when someone refers to "John 3:16," it can be easily found and referenced (go to the book of John, find the big "3" (chapter), and the small "16" (verse).

For new followers of Jesus, it is often helpful to begin by reading the Gospel of John (the story of Jesus by John–one of Jesus' twelve disciples), then the Gospel of Luke (the story of Jesus by Luke), and then the Book of Acts (the history of the early Church written by Luke). It is also helpful to begin reading in sizeable amounts that provide context but small enough amounts that provide adequate time for reflection and application. A good rule of thumb is to use the section headings of modern translations to aid in this.

As noted earlier, the Bible was written millennia ago, takes place in a very different culture, and was originally written in an ancient language. Because of this, it is highly valuable to use some secondary resources to help you read, study, and apply the Bible to your life (a Study Bible or simple Bible Commentary are great tools). As well, reading and discussing what you are learning with a more experienced believer as you begin is extremely helpful and highly recommended.

Knowing and applying the Bible in life is a needed rudder in a world of changing currents and rough seas. God wants to speak to you and guide you! As you journey with Jesus on mission, take time to regularly read the Bible, knowing that God wants to speak to you through it.

THE HOLD

Recommended Resources and Steps to Sail Further in the Voyage of Faith

1) BOOK RESOURCE: "The Map: Making the Bible Meaningful, Accessible, Practical" by Nick Page

2) ONLINE RESOURCE: Download the YouVersion App for your phone and/or tablet and use the "First Steps for New Believers" Bible reading plan. Download the Mission 119 App for your phone/tablet and use it to help you read and study the Bible.

3) ACTION STEP: Read the Gospel of John in the New Testament.

LIVING & SERVING WITH TH

One of the earliest metaphors of the Church is a boat. Several early church cathedrals were designed with images of a ship. Whether reflected through the central aisle or the vaulted ceilings which echo images of a hull, the early Church saw themselves through the image of a boat filled with God's people on His expeditionary mission.

Living with the Crew

Independence is overrated! Don't fall for the lie that God has created us to be independent. This is one of the great deceptions of our hyper-individualistic culture. We can't fulfill the great commandment to love God fully and love others alone.[31] We need other people to love and other people to love us.

---

[31] Mark 12:29-31 ""The most important one," answered Jesus, "is this: 'Hear, O Israel: The Lord our God, the Lord is one. Love the Lord your God with all your heart and with all your soul and with all your mind and with all your strength.' The second is this: 'Love your neighbour as yourself.' There is no commandment greater than these." "

Expedition: Following Jesus on a Mast-Raising, Sail-Setting, and Treasure-Seeking Journey to the Ends of the Earth

CREW

"If you want to go fast, go alone. If you want to go far, go together."

~ African Proverb

In our increasingly individualistic culture, there is a growing movement that believes people can love Jesus but not be part of the church. In counter-cultural fashion, to faithfully follow Jesus, we need to be in regular Christian community where we are committed to living and working with others on God's mission.[32]

We have been created for community. Without Christian community, we can't experience the joy and healing of confessing our sins to someone else or have them confess their sins to us.[33] We can't lay hands on each other to pray. We can't hold each other accountable.

---

[32] Hebrews 10:25 "not giving up meeting together, as some are in the habit of doing, but encouraging one another—and all the more as you see the Day approaching."

[33] James 5:16 "Therefore confess your sins to each other and pray for each other so that you may be healed. The prayer of a righteous person is powerful and effective."

We can't go to all the world alone. Community is necessary to sail the ship of faith. When the storms of life come, and they will, having others to help hold onto our mast and boom and raise our sail is vital.

We cannot follow Jesus alone. It is impossible. To believe otherwise is not just wrong, it is a dangerous and disastrous practice that will leave you without help, encouragement, guidance, and accountability. Therefore, get into community with other Jesus followers that meets regularly, enjoys life together, prays for each other, learns together, and serves together.[34] As you do, you will learn to closely follow Jesus and weather the storms of life. No one can sail an expeditionary ship alone and you need to live life with others on Jesus' mission.

Serving with the Crew

Not only do you need to be in relationship with others, you need to serve with others on Jesus' expedition. There are no passive passengers on Jesus' expeditionary vessel, just active crew members with each crew member performing an important and indispensable role for the church to successfully move forward on mission. As a follower of Jesus, you have an important part to play in the church as it fulfills God's mission.

We have been invited on a collective global expeditionary mission of love to the ends of the earth. This is not a lonely journey for a select few to pursue in isolation, but a collective adventure where we all have an important part. The Bible uses the metaphor of the Church being a body with each person being an important part.[35] Some are feet and others are arms and we need one another to effectively move forward. We each have a distinct role to fulfill in the church on Jesus' expedition.

As followers of Jesus, the Holy Spirit has entrusted each of us with at least one spiritual gift for the church to accomplish its

---

[34] Hebrews 10:25 "not giving up meeting together, as some are in the habit of doing, but encouraging one another—and all the more as you see the Day approaching."

[35] 1 Corinthians 12:27 "Now you are the body of Christ, and each one of you is a part of it."

purpose and mission.[36] When it comes to spiritual gifts, no individual is given all the gifts. The church is given all of the gifts and each follower of Jesus has been entrusted with one or more for its effective expedition together. This is part of God's gift of interdependency in community. An individual's lack of certain gifts and talents is not a deficiency to lament but a dependency to celebrate. We are created and gifted to rely on others who make us the people of God together.

If you are a follower of Jesus and don't know about spiritual gifts or what spiritual gifts have been entrusted to you, learn about them and then find a place in the church to use them. There are no passengers on Jesus' expedition – there are only crew members and each member has been given a unique role to fulfill. Discover yours today!

THE HOLD

Recommended Resources and Steps to Sail Further in the Voyage of Faith

1) BOOK RESOURCE: "Lifekeys Discovery Workbook: Discover Who You Are" by Jane Kise, David Stark, and Sandra Hirsh.

2) ONLINE RESOURCE: Discover your Spiritual Gifts by filling out a free online survey: www.giftstest.com and/or www.gifts.churchgrowth.org.

3) ACTION STEP: Find a way to serve in the church that makes use of your gifts and passions.

---

[36] 1 Corinthians 12; Romans 12; Ephesians 4

THE TREASURE-SEEKI

When I was a teen, I had the amazing opportunity to go on a sailing trip off the coast of British Columbia, Canada. My godfather, a seasoned sailor, along with his teenage son, took my brother, my father, and I on a sailing adventure. We fished, watched dolphins, and spend countless hours hanging off the edge of the ship with relentless sea-sickness.

Midway through our trip, my brother and my godfather's son went out in the Zodiac boat while we were in a narrow passage between two islands. After exploring in the Zodiac, they returned to the sailboat.

As they came alongside the ship to be picked up, we reached out for their embarkation and the Zodiac unexpectedly caught a wake and flipped. In an instant, my fun-loving godfather turned into a serious emergency rescuer. With his heart racing and searching for breath, he told my dad that he was going to turn

"If one does not know to which port one is sailing, no wind is favourable."

~ Lucius Annaeus Seneca

MISSION

the ship around but wasn't sure if we would have enough room for the ship to make the corner in the narrow straight. With wide abandon and desperation, my godfather instantly risked the cherished possession of his beloved sailboat and his personal safety to save his treasured son from eventual death in the icy cold waters of the northern pacific. In the end, we narrowly made the turn and were able to rescue them. Although extremely cold and terrified, they were safe.

When we view what is lost as treasured and worthy of our sacrifice, we move on mission with zeal and abandon. This is the picture of the Church that Jesus gives. A Church that is all in for the mission of seeking and saving the treasured lost (those who don't personally know Jesus).[37] We are invited to go on mission with our missional God who "... gave His one and only Son, that

---

[37] Luke 19:10 "For the Son of Man came to seek and to save the lost."

whoever believes in Him shall not perish but have eternal life" (John 3:16). We are invited on a rescue mission for that which is highly valued and worthy of great sacrifice and wild abandon.[38]

The Church is a rescue vessel with a mission that is more than simply proclamation of the eternal hope that is possible in Jesus. Rather, the mission of the Church is to actively seek and save the treasured lost, proclaim freedom, love the marginalized, care for the poor, show compassion, and seek justice. Therefore, once we decide to follow Jesus on His expedition, we no longer have to ask what our purpose and mission in life is. Jesus has already made that clear. We are now on a cosmic and timeless mission to follow Jesus, live boldly for Him, love lavishly and freely, and invite others to do the same.[39]

Sadly, too often, the Church is viewed by its crew as a cruise ship rather than a rescue vessel. Although the image of the Church in the Bible is of a rescue vessel that is setting the captives free, feeding the poor, and loving the marginalized, the Church has settled for an image of a cruise ship that plays shuffle board on the deck, watches a production in the theatre, and eats a leisurely meal in the dining room.[40]

As followers of Jesus, we have been saved by Jesus and empowered by the Spirit to love God and love others. May we show love and kindness to a world that is in need of it and may they look at our vessel and not see a ship of condemnation and judgment but a ship of love, humility, justice, mercy, grace and

---

[38] Luke 15

[39] Matthew 28:18-20; Acts 1:8 "But you will receive power when the Holy Spirit comes on you; and you will be my witnesses in Jerusalem, and in all Judea and Samaria, and to the ends of the earth."

[40] Mark 2:17 "On hearing this, Jesus said to them, "It is not the healthy who need a doctor, but the sick. I have not come to call the righteous, but sinners." " Luke 4:18 "The Spirit of the Lord is on me, because he has anointed me to proclaim good news to the poor. He has sent me to proclaim freedom for the prisoners and recovery of sight for the blind, to set the oppressed free." Luke 19:10 "For the Son of Man came to seek and to save the lost."

kindness that leads them aboard to participate in the same saving work that saved them.[41]

Sailing in Rough Seas

Journey with Jesus on His treasure-seeking expedition for any length of time and you will discover that the seas rarely stay still for long. Rescue ships don't avoid troubled water, they courageously set a course through it. The very nature of Jesus' expedition leads to difficult waters.

By journeying intentionally into the dark corners of our world with the light of Jesus, there will be times when the storms of grief, sickness, and death roll in from the horizon and strike with jarring force.[42] It is in these very moments when the promise of Jesus echoes amidst the dark skies, "Don't let your hearts be troubled, trust in God, and trust also in me" (John 14:1). The promise of Jesus is not that His expedition will avoid the storms but that Jesus will be with us in the midst of them. It is the promise that God will not leave us nor forsake us, and the promise that God is our ever-present help in times of trouble.[43]

Darkness and storms are on the horizon because that is the very world in which we are called to live, love, serve, and share the Good News of Jesus. Following Jesus means charting a course that leads into rough seas in the dead of night, calling us to have faith and trust in our captain who promises His peace.

---

[41] John 3:16-17 "For God so loved the world that he gave his one and only Son, that whoever believes in him shall not perish but have eternal life. For God did not send his Son into the world to condemn the world, but to save the world through him." Micah 6:8 "He has shown you, O mortal, what is good. And what does the Lord require of you? To act justly and to love mercy and to walk humbly with your God."

[42] John 16:33 "I have told you these things, so that in me you may have peace. In this world you will have trouble. But take heart! I have overcome the world."

[43] Deuteronomy 31:6 "Be strong and courageous. Do not be afraid or terrified because of them, for the Lord your God goes with you; he will never leave you nor forsake you." Hebrews 13:5 "Keep your lives free from the love of money and be content with what you have, because God has said, "Never will I leave you; never will I forsake you." " Psalm 46:1 "God is our refuge and strength, an ever-present help in trouble."

One of the most often confused realities of Jesus' expedition is the misunderstanding that the seas will somehow be calm and the journey will be void of difficulty for those who have Jesus as their captain.[44] In some church circles, it is taught that followers of Jesus will always experience excellent health, material blessings, and great popularity. Often called the "prosperity gospel", this version of Jesus' expedition is a twisted and false version of what Jesus has done and what He calls us to.

The opposite reality is equally twisted and false. This belief, taught in some church circles, is that God can't heal, that blessings can't be material, and that suffering in some way leads to salvation. This reality is also demonstrably false because Jesus can and does miraculously heal, and Jesus does, in fact, sometimes bless with material blessings or the removal of suffering. To glorify suffering is as equally damaging as denying it.

Jesus never promises to prevent storms but promises to journey with us through them, providing us comfort and peace. Jesus never promises to bless us financially but to provide for our needs in ways that fit with His will and timing. Jesus never promises our lives to be lived void of persecution or difficulty but promises to always be with us as we journey through it.[45] In fact, the Bible teaches that we can count it as pure joy when our journey takes us through turbulent waters because the storm will foster our dependence on God, grow our faith, and produce perseverance.[46]

As you follow Jesus on His expedition, the waters will not always be easy. The wind will blow, the waves will crash, and the currents will toss you, but if you keep your eyes on Jesus (who never leaves, nor forsakes) you will experience peace and joy in the midst of the most

---

[44] James 1:2-3 "Consider it pure joy, my brothers and sisters, whenever you face trials of many kinds, because you know that the testing of your faith produces perseverance."

[45] Philippians 4:4-7 "Rejoice in the Lord always. I will say it again: Rejoice! Let your gentleness be evident to all. The Lord is near. Do not be anxious about anything, but in every situation, by prayer and petition, with thanksgiving, present your requests to God. And the peace of God, which transcends all understanding, will guard your hearts and your minds in Christ Jesus."

[46] James 1:2-3 "Consider it pure joy, my brothers and sisters, whenever you face trials of many kinds, because you know that the testing of your faith produces perseverance."

Expedition: Following Jesus on a Mast-Raising, Sail-Setting, and Treasure-Seeking Journey to the Ends of the Earth

difficult storms.[47] Keep your eyes on Jesus and experience pure joy and perfect peace in the midst of our dark and stormy world.

To the Ends of the Earth

Your treasure-seeking journey will lead through difficult waters and it will always lead to the ends of the earth. Jesus' commission to the church is that we will make followers of Jesus of all nations. This is the missional heart of our missional God. With simultaneous drive, we are called to sail the expeditionary ship across our lawns, offices, and tee-boxes while also sailing across the ocean so that all people can know the good news of Jesus, experiencing new, abundant, and eternal life in Him. Jesus' expeditionary mission is both local and global and you are invited to courageously join with others in His treasure-seeking mission to the ends of the earth.

THE HOLD

Recommended Resources and Steps to Sail Further in the Voyage of Faith

1) BOOK RESOURCE: "Nudge" by Leonard Sweet. "Purple Fish: A Heart for Sharing Jesus" by Mark Wilson.

2) ONLINE RESOURCE: Learn about what God is doing around the world and how you can pray at www.operationworld.org.

3) ACTION STEP: Intentionally get to know your neighbour and practically love and serve them.

---

[47] Matthew 14:22-33

COMMISSIONING

Once a ship has been built and the crew has been gathered, it is commissioned for active duty. Often celebrated with a traditional breaking of a bottle of champagne on its hull, it is commissioned for the journey and mission ahead.

Commissioning

As a follower of Jesus, welcome to Jesus' expeditionary mission! You have been commissioned for active service. You are on a mast-raising, sail-setting, and treasure-seeking journey to the ends of the earth. There is so much to explore and the horizon is worthy of your exploration. To that end, and with your eyes fixed on Jesus, follow Him in wild abandon on the adventure of a lifetime. The sea may get rough and the sky may get dark but Jesus will never abandon ship. Jesus will guide you as you sail with Him through the darkest of storms to the ends of the earth.

> "Life is either a daring adventure or nothing at all."
>
> ~ Helen Keller

Final Port of Call

As a follower of Jesus, you also have an eternal hope with heaven as your final port of call. Whatever storms you may face or pain you may endure in this life, remember that your eternal home is secure in Jesus. Therefore, as a follower of Jesus, you no longer have to fear any of life's enemies, including death. Jesus has prepared a place for you in heaven and His final port of call has no sorrow, pain, or death.[48] Wherever your journey may take you and whatever storms you weather, know that your eternal hope is secure in Jesus as you follow Him on His great expedition.

---

[48] John 14:1-2 "Do not let your hearts be troubled. You believe in God; believe also in me. My Father's house has many rooms; if that were not so, would I have told you that I am going there to prepare a place for you?" Revelation 21:4 "He will wipe every tear from their eyes. There will be no more death or mourning or crying or pain, for the old order of things has passed away."

What Next?

As you begin your journey, commit to the following. First, surrender your life to Jesus and the work of the Holy Spirit. Although you have boarded the ship in faith and your role as a crew member is secure, the ongoing life of a crew member demands a conscious and daily surrender to the Captain. This is an ongoing process and something you must do daily. You will find yourself coming back to this time and time again. Keep raising your mast and setting your sail in surrender, submitting to the work of the Spirit. Second, begin to read your Bible daily and discover the rudder that will help guide your life. Third, begin to pray regularly, learning to realign your heart and listen to Jesus. Fourth, get into community. You need to sail with others to follow Jesus faithfully. Fifth, begin to serve in some way in the church, discovering and using the gifts that God has entrusted to you. Finally, remember that you are on a mission to love others with compassion and mercy and tell others about the hope that is within you. Motivated by love, start telling others about what Jesus has done in your life and invite them on the journey of faith with you.

Jesus' expedition is filled with risk but it is also filled with hope and adventure. Therefore, raise your mast, set your sail, and enter Jesus' treasure-seeking mission to the ends of the earth.

ABOUT THE AUTHOR

Bryce Ashlin-Mayo has been married for over twenty-five years to Laurie and they have three great kids. Bryce has served in full-time pastoral ministry with the Christian and Missionary Alliance in Canada for about twenty-five years in a variety of roles. He now serves as Lead Pastor at Westlife Church in Calgary, Alberta.

Bryce has a Bachelor of Theology from Ambrose University, Masters of Divinity in Pastoral Leadership from Taylor Seminary, and has completed his Doctorate of Ministry in Semiotics and Future Studies from George Fox University.

Bryce is passionate about seeing people come to know Jesus, filled with the Spirit, and on mission to the ends of the earth.

www.ingramcontent.com/pod-product-compliance
Lightning Source LLC
Chambersburg PA
CBHW041821040426
42453CB00005B/128